BEFORE THE WEDDING

BEFORE THE WEDDING

Questions for Muslims to Ask Before Getting Married

3rd Edition

Munira Lekovic Ezzeldine

Copyright © 2003, 2006, 2013 Munira Lekovic Ezzeldine

First Edition, 2003
Second Edition, 2006
Third Edition, 2013

Printed in the United States of America

No part of this publication may be reproduced or transmitted in any form or by any means, electronic or mechanical, including photocopying, recording, or any information storage and retrieval system now known or to be invented, without permission in writing from the author.

All rights reserved.

ISBN: 0-9742950-4-3
ISBN-13: 978-00974295046

Cover Design by Ayesha Ali

Izza Publishing ● P.O. Box 50326 ● Irvine, CA ● 92619-0326
www.beforetheweddingbook.com
info@beforetheweddingbook.com

In the Name of God, Most Gracious, Most Merciful

CONTENTS

Introduction

1	Marriage Preparation	11
2	Marrying the Right Person	17
3	The Red Flags	23
4	How to Use this Book	29
5	Personality	39
6	Islam & Culture	47
7	Finances	53
8	Life at Home	59
9	Friends & Community	65
10	Family	71
11	Children	77
12	Questions for Friends & Family	81
13	After the Wedding: Sexual Relationship	85
14	The Marriage Cycle	91
15	Intercultural & Interfaith Marriages	103

INTRODUCTION

This book speaks to the American Muslim experience where traditional cultural norms have given way to second and third-generation realities. It addresses the reality that Muslims today are finding spouses by non-traditional means. Of course, some parents still try to find spouses for their children and many continue to return to their "homeland" to find a "suitable match." Some couples meet through family networks and professional matchmakers in their community. By the same token, many Muslims are meeting in very different ways than their parents met. Young American Muslims are finding spouses on their own and through their friends. They are meeting on college campuses, at work, youth groups, Islamic events, online matching sites, and at Muslim singles events and meet-ups.

The courting process is different for different couples, but most prefer to meet a potential spouse many times and in different settings in order to get to know them better and to see how he/she relates to their family, friends and community. Some couples meet only in the presence of their parents, others meet in large groups in public, while still others meet on their own. Couples communicate over the phone, via email and in person in hopes of getting to know one another better. But if couples are meeting and conversation is taking place, why are marriages not enduring? The answer may lie in the nature of the conversation and the types of questions being asked.

While marriage is a vital aspect of Muslim life, very little education and counseling are provided for those looking to get married. The highest divorce rate in the world is found in the general U.S. population (48.6%), followed by the United Kingdom's (36%). According to Ilyas Ba-Yunus, a New York-based Muslim sociologist, the divorce rate for Muslims in North America is 33%. This means one in three Muslim marriages ends in divorce. These sobering statistics demonstrate the need to find tools for creating successful marriages. One tool may be encouraging couples to have conversations where they ask relevant and important questions which may increase their success rate in maintaining happy, healthy marriages.

BEFORE THE WEDDING

Most young Muslims in America are not prepared for marriage and are not presented opportunities to learn what factors lead to a relationship that lasts a lifetime. Marriage is not about the hype of planning a wedding or a fantasy of the perfect spouse portrayed in films and on television. Marrying "Prince Ali" or "Princess Leila" and living happily ever requires a lot of work which is not glamorous. The reality is that no one is perfect and everyone enters marriage with faults and weaknesses. While raising a family and maintaining a happy marriage can be complicated, couples can prepare themselves by developing relationship skills before getting married.

This book originated from my own experiences, first as a newlywed and then through my graduate work as a counselor in marriage and family therapy. My husband and I got to know each other for marriage by asking one another questions to determine our compatibility. We approached the process in a practical manner aimed at learning more about one-another and improving our communication. We were determined to understand one another and wanted to see if we were compatible in our values and life goals to sustain a marriage. We asked one-another many questions and after countless conversations about life goals, living standards, children and personal dreams; we developed a deep respect and admiration for one another which led us to get married.

Throughout our years of marriage, countless friends who were in the process of meeting people for marriage asked us, "What should I ask?" and "How will I know if he/she is the one?" We passed on many of the questions outlined in this book, which worked for us, as well as other questions shared with us by couples who married. Even though the courtship process is different for every Muslim couple, the focus on determining compatibility is the same for everyone.

The questions compiled in this book are by no means comprehensive, but the hope is that they will spark other questions and create space for meaningful conversations. The questions can also be revisited throughout the marriage as an ongoing tool for communication. My hope is that this book will benefit everyone, from those in the beginning stages of finding a spouse, to those who have just recently married. This book will benefit people trying to determine if someone is the right match for them, couples who are already matched but wish to explore some of their expectations before marriage, as well as newlyweds interested in developing open communication.

In this third edition of *Before the Wedding*, many revisions and additions have been made to further help you in the marriage process. Questions have been revised to be more open-ended. Included in this edition are several articles that I wrote and were originally published on www.SuhaibWebb.com that addressed the topics of red flags in a relationship" as well as who is the right person to marry. I have also included an article on intercultural and interfaith marriages and how couples can address possible stressors that may surface when creating a multicultural family. Finally, I have expanded on the chapter about the marriage cycle to give more depth to the stages and stressors all couples will face in their marriage as well as an explanation of the protective factors couples can use to establish happy and loving marriages.

1 MARRIAGE PREPARATION

"…O Allah, if you know this matter to be good for me in my faith, my livelihood and the end result of my affair, then decree it for me, make it easy for me and then bless it for me. And if you know this matter to be bad for me, my faith, my livelihood and end result of my affair, then turn it away from me and turn me away from it. Decree for me what is good, whatever it may be and then make me satisfied with it."

-Prophet Muhammad (pbuh)

In Islam, marriage preparation is multi-dimensional and it begins with a person engaging in self-reflection in order to see if they are truly ready for marriage. "Being ready" is more than just your age or financial security and must also include your emotional and developmental maturity. Possessing the ability to be unselfish and giving, as well as being sensible and responsible are required to be in a committed marital relationship.

It is advisable to make *istikhara* prayers, a prayer for guidance in important life decisions. *Istikhara* is where a person asks Allah to guide them to the best choice possible in any matter including when seeking a spouse. Building a personal relationship with Allah is vital to being a good spouse as it will purify your intentions and help you clearly understand your reasons for wanting to marry a particular person.

Additionally, any two people seeking to get married should have a *wali* (guardian) involved in the process who will guide the couple. The *wali* is usually the parents of the couple. Parents act as the advisors and mentors in the marriage process as they seek the best for their children. They share their values, expectations and boundaries for the couple in the courting process. Even Muslims who have non-Muslim parents should nonetheless consult their parents and involve them in the courting process. However, if non-Muslim parents are unreceptive to Islam, it is suggested that the person ask their *imam* (religious leader) for guidance. Respect for elders is paramount in Islam and considering their advice when selecting a spouse is essential.

Marriage is the union of more than just two individuals; it is the bringing together of two unique families, and thus the process needs to include both parents. The couple that goes through the series of questions outlined in this book should do so with the knowledge of their guardians, because a secret relationship between a man and woman should not exist before marriage. Additionally, a couple should not be completely alone with one another before marriage because this would be considered *khulwa*. This is when a single man and single woman are completely alone together where no one can see them, thereby tempting them to commit fornication. Having conversations in public spaces will help eliminate any potential crossing of Islamic boundaries. A couple should always act with respect and modesty toward one another in their words and actions. A person's character is demonstrated by the self-control exhibited while interacting with others and especially when speaking with a potential spouse.

Other ways couples can understand the realities of marriage is by attending marriage preparation courses and reading books about marriage which can help them develop healthy relationship skills. Additionally, seeking pre-marital counseling is extremely beneficial for new couples. The most successful pre-marital counseling program that exists for Muslims in the U.S. was established by Imam Mohamed Magid of the All Dulles Area Muslim Society (ADAMS) in Northern Virginia. Imam Magid is a pioneer in requiring couples to undergo counseling prior to officiating their marriage. Today, numerous Muslim counselors exist throughout the U.S. for couples to meet with before getting married and many imams are encouraging couples to seek pre-marital counseling before writing the marriage contract. *Insha'Allah (God-willing)*, more religious leaders will take Imam Magid's lead and help implement pre-marital counseling in their mosques and communities.

The purpose of pre-marital counseling is to help a couple assess strengths and areas of growth in the relationship as well as teach them communication and conflict resolution skills. In counseling, couples can clarify their expectations and roles in the marriage as well as strengthen their commitment to one another. A counselor does not determine a couple's compatibility. Rather the role of a counselor is to help couples explore their dynamic so they can evaluate their relationship when making the decision to marry.

Outside of counseling, Muslims continue to address pre-marital concerns by familiarizing themselves with a person directly as well as indirectly through family and friends. Many times these conversations and meetings are ineffective because couples do not know how to determine if they are a good match and may even be hesitant to talk about certain difficult topics. Some topics may be quickly brushed over and many questions may never be asked. Ultimately, asking thoughtful and relevant questions will help deepen conversations in order for a couple to better understand one another and make a more informed decision about marriage.

The purpose of the questions in this book is to help couples better understand each other but also to better understand themselves. By asking and answering questions, you will have greater self-awareness, will establish positive communication skills and begin the work of building a lasting marriage. *Insha'Allah*, you and your potential spouse will discuss these questions thoughtfully and honestly with one another as you determine your compatibility.

2 MARRYING THE RIGHT PERSON

"... women of purity are for men of purity, and men of purity are for women of purity: these are not affected by what people say: for them there is forgiveness and a provision honorable."

Qur'an (24:26)

Am I marrying the right person? This is the question a person must ask before marrying someone. While many factors are used to determine compatibility, you may be surprised to read that the answer to this question is in fact mostly based on feelings. Through the process of getting to know different types of people, you will discover a variety of personalities and, more importantly, the type of person you are most comfortable being around. Over time, and with increased maturity, you will also develop a deeper understanding of your own personality. Eventually, you will meet someone you feel compatible with and want to consider for marriage. You will inevitably ask, "Is this the right person for me?" As described to us in the Qur'an (24:26) a reminder that people are matched. The following is a description of the feelings necessary to know that you have found *your* match.

The right person is someone you feel comfortable opening up to – someone you can be vulnerable with. The right person encourages you to make decisions that are right for you. This may include decisions around a healthy lifestyle and supporting your efforts to find balance between work and family. You feel encouraged and supported to grow in all areas of your life because the person you want to marry is not negative, selfish or critical. Rather, when you are with this person you feel safe to share your thoughts and ideas and you feel uplifted by their support. The right person is someone you have developed a friendship with and you mutually enjoy each other's company. Building a marriage on a friendship is important because love grows out of friendship.

You and the right person for you have similar life goals and values. This doesn't mean your goals and values are exactly the same, but they don't contradict. You are able to agree on long term goals that you can attain together. When you are with the right person, you are able to communicate your feelings and concerns and you don't feel that you need to keep them bottled up inside. When you disagree on something, you are both able to share and listen to each other's opinions, then you both seek compromise. Conversations with the right person are interesting and help you grow intellectually. With the right person you are comfortable sharing your thoughts and feelings on various topics. Couples naturally grow and change throughout the course of their marriage and this requires an ability to effectively communicate and resolve concerns as they come up.

The right person is kind, considerate, and polite to you and the people around you – and *not* just to impress you. This person encourages you to have good relationships with your family and friends. Marriage is the bringing together of two families, not becoming an isolated couple. These behaviors toward your friends and family are a natural reflection of a person's true character. Showering only *you* with kindness but not extending this to your friends and family is a sign of inconsistent character. Character is shown through the actions that come to us naturally – whenever and to whomever. Both you and the person you want to marry will *show* character through what comes naturally more than anything that will ever be *said*. The person who is right for you isn't rude, childish, arrogant or selfish. Rather, they are thoughtful and caring of everyone around them, not only their parents and their boss but the waiter and the clerk. A marriage is built on the feelings of respect and compassion and unless these come naturally, whatever behaviors are used to impress you before marriage will not last the everyday interactions of a marriage.

Finally, the right person is honest with you and is someone you can trust. This person is truthful with you about life decisions. The person you want to marry doesn't seek to control your life but rather seeks to share a life with you. The right person trusts you and doesn't scrutinize you or make you justify your every move. When you are with the right person, you will feel completely safe and accepted for who you are. You will feel you can share your mistakes and work on your weaknesses. It must be said that anyone who is dishonest or does things that are against your values is someone you should not marry. The foundation of a healthy marriage is one that is based on honesty and trust between two partners.

Establishing compatibility for marriage is based on many factors and the most obscure – yet most important – are the feelings we have about the person. There are some people we instantly "click" with and there are others we find interesting and want to learn more about. These are the initial feelings, but as we get to know someone and seek to find compatibility in values and goals, one must carefully examine their feelings. Being with the right person is uplifting to our spirit and the relationship brings us tranquility as is best described in surah 30, verse 21: "… *And among His Signs is this, that He created for you mates from among yourselves, that ye may dwell in tranquility with them, and He has put love and mercy between your (hearts): verily in that are Signs for those who reflect.*" While no human being is perfect and we should not be looking for unrealistic qualities, you will know if you have found the person that is a good match for you. Remember that finding the right person is only half the challenge, you must first *be* the right person.

Munira Lekovic Ezzeldine, "Am I Marrying the Right Person?" www.suhaibwebb.com. Copyright © 2010-2013. All rights reserved. Reproduced with permission.

3   THE RED FLAGS

"A good marriage is one which allows for change and growth in the individuals and in the way they express their love."

-Pearl Buck

Getting to know someone for marriage can be a nerve-racking and exciting experience all at the same time. Through conversations, a couple seeks to learn about each other and determine compatibly for a lifetime together. However, many couples get so emotionally attached in the early stages of the relationship that they cannot see or choose to deny red flags that arise. Being self-reflective and in tune with your feelings is important in identifying potential problems in a relationship. Divorcees and married couples with significant problems always cite early signs or red-flags that they did not realize were important or did not know would have a major impact on the relationship. Red flags are signs that something is not sitting well with an individual and can become a source of conflict within the marriage. Not all problems before marriage are signs of a doomed relationship. Some issues that arise before marriage can be discussed and compromises can be made. Open communication and problem solving are foundational to a healthy, successful and happy marriage. It must be said that there are some problems or red flags that indicate deeper personal issues that can only be addressed through individual or pre-marital counseling.

Communication before marriage is vital because it is the only way you can connect with a potential spouse and understand his or her viewpoints. Communication is not only about the ability to talk, it is also about the ability to listen. Red flags in this area of the relationship are that you do not feel like your potential spouse understands you, nor seeks to understand what is important to you in your life. If your feelings are dismissed or you are constantly being cut off, then you may be considering someone for marriage who is not a good listener and is not in tune with the feelings of others. Also, being criticized and/or spoken to sarcastically are signs of disrespect. This is a problem because mutual respect between spouses is the cornerstone of a successful marriage.

On the other hand you may feel like thoughts and feelings are shared and heard, but your potential spouse does not share his or her own views and feelings. This may be an indication that your potential spouse is emotionally unavailable and not ready for the emotional attachment required in a marriage. A requirement for a successful marriage is that each spouse is emotionally ready to be vulnerable and intimate with another human being.

The way a couple communicates and resolves conflicts are important aspects to consider before marriage. If a couple is constantly arguing and leaves arguments unresolved then they face serious problems in a marital relationship. If you find yourself consciously avoiding certain topics out of a fear of your potential spouse's reaction, then you are not being fully honest in the relationship. In order to be in an authentic marriage, each spouse must be able to be his or her true self and not shy away from discussing difficult topics.

A potential spouse that expresses extreme emotions, such as uncontrollable anger, excessive fear or irrational jealousy is a major concern because these could be signs of an abusive partner. A person that tries to control and manipulate another person's behavior, such as how to dress, how to interact with family and friends, how to live, etc. all signify that this person desires power in the relationship. When getting to know one another, couples usually mistake this classic red flag as a sign of care and concern rather than a pattern toward an emotionally or even physically abusive relationship. A potential spouse who is unable to resolve conflicts, admit mistakes, or deal with constructive criticism is likely to be someone who is not able to take personal responsibility in their life. All of these personal issues are signs that the individual is in need of personal growth and change before attempting to have a healthy marital relationship.

The adage "actions speak louder than words" cannot be truer than when observing the behavior of a potential spouse. Lack of consistency between what a person says and does is a red flag that the individual cannot be trusted and/or that there are major character flaws. In addition, if your potential spouse says and does things that do not reflect your own values, this is a wakeup call that you may not be compatible. Any pattern of dishonesty, rationalizing questionable behavior, or twisting words to his or her benefit is a red flag that the individual has difficulty with personal responsibility and needs time and support to mature emotionally.

Many times, problems in marriages arise because of in-laws and couples do not pay attention to the early predictors of these issues. A potential spouse that is overly dependent on parents for finances, decision-making and/or emotional security is someone who may not be ready to get married. A potential spouse who is in an overly dependent family relationship will have difficulty moving into an interdependent relationship with a spouse. While it is of course natural that both families remain connected to the new couple, the shift to *emotional* independence from the family is a growth process that is necessary so that the new couple can begin creating their own life together.

Trusting your intuition and addressing uneasy feelings that arise during the process of getting to know someone is important. Intuition is your compass and is alerting you that something may be wrong in the relationship with your potential spouse. One must find the courage to follow this intuition. To continue getting to know someone or proceed toward marriage with these uncertainties can be disastrous. Many choose to ignore the red flags out of a fear of hurting a person's feelings or what the family and community may say. Getting married out of a fear of letting others down or feeling pressured are signs that the relationship is unstable and the foundation for a healthy marriage is unstable. In order to be in a healthy marriage, individuals need to grow up and grow emotionally before they can be in a relationship with another individual. No one is perfect, but each individual has a responsibility to work on his or her own personal issues and flaws. As ibn Arabi says, "He who knows himself knows his Lord." Self-reflection is vital to help you understand yourself, your relationship with others and ultimately help bring you closer to Allah.

Munira Lekovic Ezzeldine, "Reading the Red Flags" www.suhaibwebb.com. Copyright © 2010-2013. All rights reserved. Reproduced with permission.

4   HOW TO USE THIS BOOK

"He is the One who created you from a single soul, and from that created a spouse, that he might find comfort in her."

Qur'an (7:189)

This book is a guide, not an instruction manual. Discussing the questions in this book is a process, not a one day marathon. When asking these questions, you should not make the other person feel like they are being interrogated or going through an intense exam. While the questions are a means of getting to know a person, they should be asked in an environment of respect and pure intentions. They should not be treated as a checklist, but instead, should serve as the material for an on-going conversation rooted in patience and honesty.

Many of the questions in this book will be

difficult to ask as well as answer. However, the key to success is to answer them truthfully. The questions are not intended to reveal private and destructive details from the past. Despite being personal, they are all relevant and purposeful. You will need to use your discretion regarding the proper time and stage in your relationship to ask them.

When asking the questions, you should not seek to find out what is "wrong" with a person but rather to reveal his/her character and the potential for a lifetime together. Your goal should be to find someone who answers the questions in a way that you respect and can live with. There is no *right* answer to any question, only an answer that is *right for you*. The right answer will depend on your values and your upbringing. By going through the process, you will begin to understand one another's views, where you agree and disagree and where you will need to compromise.

Asking questions does not replace the intuition one may gain through simple observation, but it does help you see the bigger picture. As you begin to get to know a person for marriage, you will have disagreements and discover areas for improvement as well as uncover issues for further discussion. To find a compatible spouse you must identifying the core qualities you find most important with your lifestyle. Some answers will align with your goals, values and lifestyle while others will not. On issues with no compromise, you will have to examine whether you can maintain your convictions without controlling your potential spouse's way of life. Realistically some issues will arise in any exchange between two people before deciding to get married – do not ignore them. Addressing them as they arise will help you prevent "surprises" later in the relationship.

Answer those questions that you are willing to answer, but also pay attention to questions you have difficulty discussing or even refuse to discuss. Be aware of patterns in your (and your potential spouse's) discomfort because they may indicate incompatibility. Finally, pay attention not only to what the other person says but to how they react to questions.

Follow your gut. Pay attention when a question or answer creates a knot in your stomach. These feelings will tell you something about what you value and expect in marriage and what you are hearing from your potential spouse. Beyond the words being said, you should also listen to the bigger message that communicates a person's values, prejudices, past experiences and future goals. These are all revealed in the way a person communicates. You should listen carefully to a person's words, jokes, comments and complaints, from which you can discover patterns indicative of deep-rooted beliefs and behaviors. Some people easily agree only to criticize later. Others are sweet about everything which later makes you question their sincerity. Still others use jokes, sarcasm and teasing as a means of communication. Whatever it may be, you must decide if you are comfortable with the way ideas are communicated, and if each of you is being correctly understood by the other.

Knowing a person "well enough" for marriage is very subjective, but the more you know beforehand, the less likely you are to discover qualities, behaviors or values that you cannot live with after the wedding. The decision to marry someone should not be based solely on emotions. Becoming emotionally invested in a person may cause you to excuse every element of incompatibility which could cause you to enter into an unhappy marriage. Does this mean you should never be emotionally invested with someone before marriage? Of course not, however, it is more realistic to say that you should always strive to evaluate your potential spouse without being blinded by your emotions.

When determining if you are marrying the right person, you should ask yourself, "Can I accept my potential spouse just as they are?" Expecting him/her to change for you or others is unrealistic. People may choose to change something about themselves, but only when it is significant to them and when they are ready to, not at the request or expectation of others. Your decision to marry must be based on what *is*, not on what *might* be. Accepting both the strengths and weaknesses in your potential spouse without an expectation for change is key.

It may feel as though the process of discovering compatibility goes quickly and is inundated with emotion. At times it can be overwhelming, confusing and complicated. For this reason, a special section after each chapter entitled "Take a Moment" has been added. When you complete a chapter, look back at any notes you've taken and then be alone for a moment to reflect on what you have learned about yourself, your potential spouse and the feelings you have at the moment. These notes will be helpful for you to refer back to as you approach a final decision.

Since family and friends sometimes push marriage without allowing for sufficient introspection, these first set of questions will help you begin the self-reflection process. These initial questions will help you discover and establish your expectations which is part of determining your values and beliefs. While self-reflecting, you will need to think honestly about how you are versus how you want to be perceived. Remember that you are not just trying to impress – you are trying to find someone you can live with, have children with and build a life with. Once you have greater self-awareness, you will be in a better position to determine how compatible another person is with your values and beliefs. You should go through all the questions in the book yourself before asking them and select your core non-negotiable questions, the ones that would essentially determine character and compatibility. Knowing yourself will be your compass in the journey of getting to know someone for marriage.

TAKE A MOMENT

1. What are your personal set of values in life? Identify your top ten core values.

   _____

   _____

   _____

   _____

   _____

   _____

   _____

2. Why do you feel you are ready to get married?

   _____

   _____

   _____

   _____

3. What do you think are your responsibilities in a marriage?

4. What core qualities are you looking for in a spouse?

5. What character qualities are you not willing to accept in a spouse?

6. What are your expectations for marriage?

5 PERSONALITY

"Success in marriage is much more than finding the right person; it is a matter of being the right person."

Arabian Proverb

While initial conversations are packed with personal questions, a personality slowly shows over time. Sociability, organization, flexibility, cooperation and resilience are all part of a personality that are unique to each individual. Personalities are constant over time and something each person develops from early childhood. The questions in this chapter have been divided into categories including education, profession, personality and past experiences. These will give you a general overview of a person's traits and ambitions which will highlight their character.

By answering these questions, you will be able

to determine if there is an intellectual connection and whether you can engage in thought-provoking conversations with your potential spouse. You will discuss your educational background and the value you place on learning and seeking knowledge. Attitudes about education can affect your marriage because if one or both of you want to continue your education, having a supportive spouse will be essential. A lack of support for your goals may mean you are unable to fulfill your personal or professional ambitions which can cause problems in a marriage.

Work is an important area to discuss because it will affect the amount of stress a spouse brings home, the amount of free time he/she will have, income level and general happiness. Also, an individual's personality can be wrapped up in what they do, since they are at work for a least one-third of the day. By discussing your professions it will help you understand and support your potential spouse's profession and the demands of their work schedule. For example, someone who is self-employed has irregular hours and may be more occupied with work than someone who leaves work behind at the end of a long day.

Additionally, you will be able to determine if your goals for the future intersect. Exploring your vision of the future is as valuable, if not more valuable, than reviewing past events, because the future is what you will have to share. You should also discuss events from the past that may have an impact on the marriage. Discussing the past may be difficult for some, but it is a useful tool in understanding why a person believes and behaves the way they do. It should be done gradually and with compassion. More importantly, remember that a person's beliefs now are more important than what happened in the past.

Education

1. How much education have you completed? How highly do you value education?

2. Do you plan to seek further education? What is your goal?

3. Would you consider traveling to another country for education or employment? Where? When? For how long?

Profession

4. Where are you employed and how long do you see yourself there?

5. What are your professional goals and ambitions for the next 10 years?

6. How much time do you spend working each week? How will this change when you get married?

7. How do you prioritize work and family?

Personality

8. Do you consider yourself an introvert or an extrovert? What does this mean to you?

9. What is one good quality you see in yourself? One bad quality?

10. What are some qualities you are looking for in a spouse?

11. Which topics do you feel qualified to give advice about?

12. How do you make decisions for yourself - logic, intuition or indecisive?

13. What do you value most in your life?

14. What do you believe will never change about you?

15. How do you feel about making changes for your spouse or a relationship?

16. What do you consider quality time? What do you consider a waste of time?

17. Have you ever gotten into a physical fight? Has anyone ever had reason to be afraid of you?

18. Is it ever appropriate for someone to express anger in a physical way? If so, when and how?

19. When was the last time you were angry? What did you do about it?

20. What would you fight for (literally and figuratively)?

21. What makes you jealous?

22. How do you express honesty? When is it appropriate not to be honest?

23. How do you feel about teasing and sarcasm?

24. Do you tend to trust people? Are you cautious or suspicious? Why?

25. What things are you particular about being done in a certain way? What annoys you?

26. How do you apologize for your mistakes? Do you tend to blame others?

27. If you can see that you are wrong, do you hold onto your position or can you change your mind?

28. How comfortable are you with disagreements? How do you resolve conflicts?

29. What do you feel are acceptable grounds for a couple to divorce? If problems develop in your marriage, would you be willing to go to marriage counseling?

30. Do you have any physical or mental health concerns? Are there any health problems that run in your family?

Past Experiences

31. Have you been engaged or married before? If so, how has that experience influenced your present feelings about marriage?

32. Over the last five years, how do you think you have changed for the better? For the worse?

33. What five things have you done in your life that you are most proud of?

34. What about your past should I know about?

TAKE A MOMENT

1. What did you learn about yourself?

_____

_____

_____

_____

_____

_____

_____

2. What did you learn about your potential spouse?

_____

_____

_____

_____

_____

_____

6   ISLAM & CULTURE

"Life has taught us that love does not consist in gazing at each other but in looking outward together in the same direction."

-Antoine De Saint-Exupery

Your core values and beliefs should be central to your conversation about Islam and culture in order to help you understand how you both view the world and yourselves in it. The following questions are vital because they will provide a deeper understanding of how the other person thinks and comes to conclusions, based on their beliefs. Innate beliefs are the core of a person's being and what they live by, which also means they usually have the least room for compromise. Also, when it comes to core beliefs, it is important to see whether what is being said is being practiced and lived.

Finding a spouse with the same beliefs and values will make a marriage easier and help you grow together spiritually. Differences in application and interpretation of Islam can be managed if both people are open-minded enough to accept one another's right to their beliefs, and do not expect their spouse to do things their way. It is important to determine the importance of Islam in each other's lives because this will affect how you each make life decisions, raise children, solve problems and fulfill your religious obligations. Differences in interpretation and application of Islam must be communicated.

Since everyone differs in their degree of religious practice, you should clearly express your beliefs and boundaries to your potential spouse. There are diverse applications of Islam, and Muslims live within their own spectrum of understanding and interpretation. A spouse who devalues your practice of Islam or even your culture can lead to conflict in the relationship. Understanding and respecting the role religion and culture play in your spouse's life will give you greater insight into their worldview.

1. How do you primarily self-identify (i.e. by nationality, race, religion, family, etc.)?

2. How strongly do you identify with your ethnic/cultural background?

3. Were you raised with a particular culture? How do you practice your culture?

4. What aspects of your culture are different from Islam? Are these important to you?

5. Were you raised as a practicing Muslim? If not, when and what was your turning point?

6. If you were always practicing Islam, what shaped you into the Muslim you are today?

7. Do you subscribe to any particular *mad'hab* (school of thought), sect, group, or leader? How important is this in your life and how important will this be in your family's life?

8. How do you address differing interpretations of Islam?

9. Which Muslim groups and/or organizations are you a part of? If not a part of any, are there any you support or oppose?

10. Which cultural or non-Muslim groups and/or organizations are you a part of?

11. What does volunteering/activism mean to you? Are you involved in your community?

12. How much time do you spend doing Islamic volunteer work? How will this change when you get married?

13. Do you believe in voting and involvement in the political process?

14. How do you feel about women in leadership positions?

15. How do you feel about a woman wearing or not wearing the *hijab* (head scarf)?

16. What are your thoughts on polygamy?

17. How do you feel about attending the mosque? How often do you attend?

18. How do you feel about attending religious classes or lessons?

19. Do you fast, pray and give *zakat* (almsgiving)? How important are these to you?

20. How do you feel about praying in public? Do you pray at work/school?

21. Have you made *Hajj* (pilgrimage) or '*Umrah* (minor pilgrimage)? When do you see yourself going in the future?

22. Are you interested in learning the classical Arabic language? Why or why not?

23. What type of relationship do you have or would you like to have with the Qur'an?

24. How accepting are you of people with other religious beliefs? Are you involved in inter-faith work?

25. What kinds of relationships do you have with your non-Muslim friends and co-workers?

26. What goals do you have for self-improvement and spiritual growth?

27. How do you think being married will bring you closer to Allah?

28. What does spirituality mean to you?

TAKE A MOMENT

1. What did you learn about yourself?

___

2. What did you learn about your potential spouse?

___

7 FINANCES

"You give but little when you give of your possessions. It is when you give of yourself that you truly give."

-Khalil Gibran

Finances can be a major stressor for couples and it is one of the leading causes for couples to divorce. It is vital that you understand one another's expectations about how you each envision making and spending money. Once married, your financial life will no longer be your own personal domain because you will share your wealth and/or debt with someone else. Investments you make, homes you choose, even employment decisions will become decisions for both of you since you will have to share financial responsibilities. These views and expectations must be articulated clearly in order to understand your financial compatibility and to avoid unexpected surprises.

Money is an important topic of discussion because an individual's views about money are based on their life experiences. Few people like to talk about their money habits, but money explains many underlying values a person holds. Some people are consumed by money while others struggle to save and manage money. Due to the sensitivity around the subject, questions about money and a person's income should not be asked in the first few conversations with someone because no one wants to feel they are being selected or denied because of their financial status. So use sensibility and compassion when approaching this subject.

1. What standard of living are you currently used to? What standard of living did your parents provide you when growing up? (i.e. type of house, car, etc.)?

2. What is the earning potential in your present career?

3. What are your long-term financial goals and how do you see them being achieved?

4. What is your perception of the wife's financial role (in terms of profession, home, family)? What is your perception of the husband's financial role?

5. Do you believe in keeping money in separate bank accounts or a joint account?

6. If the wife works, should she contribute her income to the joint account or her own personal account?

7. What do you do with your money (i.e. spend, invest, save, etc.)?

8. Are you comfortable with bank interest? Stock market? Insurance? Mortgage?

9. Have you ever been bankrupt?

10. What are your beliefs and practices about using credit cards?

11. Do you consider yourself thrifty or extravagant when spending? What stores do you typically shop at? How often do you shop?

12. What are your priorities when spending? How much on average do you spend each month on food, clothes, hobbies, entertainment and home decor?

13. How much do you currently have in outstanding debts (i.e. student loans, car payments, mortgage, etc.)?

14. How much money do you need to make to support your current lifestyle?

15. How will you and your spouse decide to spend money? Which types of purchases would be joint decisions and individual decisions?

16. Will you go shopping with your spouse for clothes, food, electronics, etc.? Why or why not?

17. Who currently manages your finances? Are you comfortable with how your money is managed?

18. How do you feel about loaning and/or borrowing money from friends and family?

19. Which charity organizations do you support with your money and/or time?

TAKE A MOMENT

1. What did you learn about yourself?

___

2. What did you learn about your potential spouse?

___

8 LIFE AT HOME

"…They (your spouses) are your garments and you are their garments…"

Qur'an (2:187)

Home is the place where people retreat to, in order to escape from the demands of the world. The type of home a person was raised in will undoubtedly influence their expectations and desires for what they envision for their own home once married. For instance, a person who has always lived in a house may expect to move into a house after marriage or when they have children. Conversely, a person who has always lived in an apartment or rental home, may find no value in buying a home. These types of expectations need to be articulated so that there is a common understanding.

Learning to live with another human being who does not know your habits and routines is a big transition for any new couple and cannot be fully understood before marriage. Many of these questions will make you feel like you are interviewing for a roommate, but discussing these questions will help you establish a mutual understanding of what kind of home life each of you envisions. Incompatibility with views on household issues and personal habits can lead to frustration in a marriage. Therefore, knowing one another's preferences, working out agreements and being tolerant of habits will make the transition to married life smoother.

1. What is your preference in terms of the location or type of home you want to live in?

2. Where do you consider home? In which country/state/city do you want to live in the short-term? Long-term?

3. Which geographical location do you see yourself living in (i.e. city, suburb, etc.)?

4. How do you see your lifestyle in the future (i.e. working class, middle class, upper class)?

5. Have you always lived with your parents? Have you ever lived alone or with roommates?

6. How much privacy do you need in your home? Do you need space that is exclusively yours?

7. Would the person you live with now describe you as neat, tidy, messy or dirty?

8. Who do you feel is responsible for decorating the home? Who was responsible in your parents' home?

9. Who do you feel is responsible for cleaning the home? Making repairs in the home? Who was responsible in your parents' home?

10. Do you smoke cigarettes? In the home?

11. Do you have pets? Who cares for them? Do you want pets?

12. What sort of bad habits do you have that might affect your spouse?

13. Can you cook? Who do you feel is responsible for cooking? Grocery shopping?

14. Do you prefer eating in a restaurant or eating home-made food?

15. What type of food do you like and generally eat? What will you not eat? Do you only eat *zabiha* (slaughtered by Islamic standards)?

16. Are you a day or night person?

17. What time do you like to go to sleep and wake-up each day?

TAKE A MOMENT

1. What did you learn about yourself?

_____

_____

_____

_____

_____

_____

2. What did you learn about your potential spouse?

_____

_____

_____

_____

_____

_____

9   FRIENDS & COMMUNITY

"Let there be spaces in your togetherness."

-Kahlil Gibran

Friendships can be tied around many different things (mosque, sports, work, university). You and your potential spouse will come from an existing group of friends, which may or may not overlap. How you will each interact with one another's friends and how you will make new friends as a couple is something interesting to explore. Take a careful look at who your potential spouse's friends are and how much of an influence they have. You can develop greater understanding of people by the type of friends they have. If you do not feel comfortable around his/her friends, then you should explore why that is and how that will change once you are married.

Additionally, leisure time and holidays are explored to help you understand the impact your social life will have on your marriage as well as the inevitable shift that will occur. You should be comfortable with how you each envision spending free time and holidays as a couple. Understanding what each of you likes doing in your free time and what activities you would enjoy doing together is important. For example, you may both enjoy going to the movies for fun but other activities you may enjoy doing separately, like watching sports, going hiking, etc. Leisure activities can have a great impact on your marriage, not only in terms of what you do together, but the respect you show for each other's interests.

1. Describe your best friend.

2. Are your friends primarily married or single? How will this affect your married life?

3. How are you and your friends similar? Which of your friends has had the biggest influence on you?

4. Do you enjoy spending time with others or being alone? How would this change after you get married?

5. How do you feel about your spouse having friends or co-workers of the opposite sex?

6. Are you comfortable shaking hands with the opposite sex?

7. What types of gatherings are you most comfortable with? Do you prefer getting together with a small group of friends or a large group?

8. When you have friends over, do you prefer to have everyone sit together or separated by gender?

9. Are the people you surround yourself with mostly like you or different than you?

10. What ethnicity/nationality/religion do your closest friends identify with?

11. Which of your friends will have the most frequent interaction and/or biggest influence on your family?

12. Describe the community you were raised in as a child and your fondest memories.

13. How do you celebrate *Eid al-Fitr* and *Eid al-Adha*? How will this change when you get married?

14. How do you celebrate birthdays and/or anniversaries? Do you celebrate any other religious or non-religious holidays? How important are these to you?

15. What holidays and events do you envision spending with your parents, siblings and/or friends? Would this change with marriage? With children?

16. What activities do you like to do in your free time for fun? How often?

17. Do you enjoy physical fitness? In what ways do you work to maintain your physical health?

18. How would you resolve a situation where your spouse enjoyed or wanted to participate in an activity you did not enjoy?

19. What do you like to do when you go on vacation? What would be your dream vacation?

20. Do you like to travel? Where have you traveled?

21. How do you feel about your spouse traveling alone for business/pleasure? Is there any distance that is too far?

TAKE A MOMENT

1. What did you learn about yourself?

2. What did you learn about your potential spouse?

10 FAMILY

"The goal in marriage is not to think alike but to think together."

-Robert Dodds

While getting to know your potential spouse, ensure you are comfortable with each other's family by meeting each other's parents and siblings multiple times. Keeping family involved in the courting process will make the transition to marriage smoother as everyone learns more about one another. Understanding the family that your potential spouse comes from is important as well as reflecting on your own family and how they will influence your marital relationship. Family relationships express how you each value connections with the closest people in your life.

Most people develop their first understanding of

relationship skills from their families and what they saw role modeled. Your relationship with your potential spouse can be influenced by the type of relationship you have with your family. Any existing conflicts you have with family members may also impact your relationship. Respecting and valuing relationships with family is important since these are the people who helped to nurture the growth and development of both of you. These questions will help you understand the relationships you each have with your families and how those relationships have influenced your values, beliefs and choices.

1. Where does your family live? How long have your parents lived in this country/state/city?

2. Are your parents Muslims? How do they practice Islam?

3. What culture are your parents? What defines their culture (i.e. food, clothing, holidays, language, family-structure, etc.)?

4. How do your parents differentiate between their culture and Islam?

5. Are all your parents' closest friends from the same culture?

6. What language do you speak with your family at home?

7. What qualities do your parents expect in your future spouse?

8. How does your family feel about you marrying someone from a different background?

9. What do you like about your family? What do you dislike about your family?

10. What is your relationship like with your parents?

11. How do you feel about living close to parents?

12. What is your relationship like with your sibling(s)? How has the relationship changed?

13. What type of things do your parents argue about? How do they resolve conflicts? What do they do when they get angry?

14. What have you learned from you parents' relationship?

15. How involved do you feel your parents should be in your marriage?

16. Describe your mother and father. In what ways are you like each of them? In what ways are you different?

17. How often do you communicate with your parents? How often do you visit your parents and

siblings? How would this change when you get married? When you have children?

18. How do you feel about having your parents move in with you once they reach old age? Your spouse's parents?

19. How do you feel about relatives or friends living in your home for an extended period of time (i.e. months, years)?

20. Have you ever or would you ever break off relations with a family member? Would your parents?

21. Who in your family do you go to for advice?

22. What does "obedience" to your parents mean to you? Do you find it difficult to say "no" to your parents?

23. Does your family keep secrets? Are there any you are still holding that would affect your marriage?

24. Do you believe a wife should change her last name to her husband's? Explain why or why not.

TAKE A MOMENT

1. What did you learn about yourself?

2. What did you learn about your potential spouse?

11 CHILDREN

"The most important thing a father can do is love their mother."

-Theodore Hesburgh

Choosing a spouse is not only choosing a life partner, but also choosing a future parent and role model for your children. Having compatible ideas of how you each envision raising and caring for your children will help clarify your long term goals once you are married. These questions will help you explore how you were each raised and what ideals you have about raising your own children.

1. Do you want to have children? If so, how many? When would you like to start a family?

2. What aspects of parenting do you feel are the mother's/father's responsibilities?

3. Do you feel that one or both parents should take time away from their careers to raise children?

4. How do you feel about putting your child in daycare? preschool?

5. Do you want your children to attend public school, private school, Islamic school or homeschool? How important is this to you?

6. What would you do if your spouse could not have children? Would you consider adoption?

7. What would you do if your child was born with a disability?

8. How do you think you will discipline your children? How did your parents discipline you?

9. Do you believe boys should be raised differently than girls? Why?

10. If you have a daughter, will you want her to wear *hijab* (headscarf)? If so, at what age?

11. Do you feel your parents raised you differently than your sibling(s)?

12. What do you feel is the most important thing to teach your children?

13. What culture do you want your children to adopt? How will you share culture with your children?

14. How will you teach faith to your children? How did your parents teach faith to you?

15. What do you envision as quality time with your children?

16. How did your parents raise you? How will you raise your children similarly? Differently?

TAKE A MOMENT

1. What did you learn about yourself?

___

2. What did you learn about your potential spouse?

___

12 QUESTIONS FOR FRIENDS & FAMILY

"He who asks the questions cannot avoid the answers."

-Cameroon Proverb

People are best understood in relation to their closest friends and family. It is advisable that you talk to at least two people who are very close to your potential spouse. These two contacts should be people who have lived with or known your potential spouse for a long period of time.

According to renowned scholar Imam Nawawi, discussing information for business or marriage is not considered backbiting and it is a duty upon the person being asked to be completely open and honest when sharing information about a potential spouse. Concealing information about a person is inappropriate in the context of a possible marriage because it does not allow the opportunity to make an informed decision for marriage.

When asking these close friends or family members' questions, do not be embarrassed or shy, and remember to ask for specific examples. Also, do not preoccupy yourself with ancient history. While the past has an impact, it should not be the only factor when deciding to marry. Marriage is one of life's most important decisions and you are seeking information to make an informed decision The reality is that the truth about someone will eventually come out and it is better if honest answers are given before a marriage takes place.

1. How long have you known him/her?

2. Do you think he/she is ready to get married? Why or why not?

3. What type of person do you think would be compatible with him/her?

4. What are his/her best qualities? Worst qualities?

5. If you had a brother/sister, would you recommend him/her? Why or why not?

6. Give me a specific example of when this person dealt with anger and/or frustration. What was his/her method of coping?

7. On what subjects have you disagreed with him/her in the past?

8. Who does he/she rely on when making decisions?

9. Describe the role Islam & culture plays in his/her life.

10. Do you see him/her as helpful? generous? responsible? Give examples.

11. How does he/she react when they do not get their own way?

12. How would you describe this person's role in his/her family? With friends? In the community?

13. How good is he/she at keeping promises?

14. How does he/she relate to the opposite gender? Do they have many friends?

15. What types of people does he/she not get along with? Why?

TAKE A MOMENT

1. What did you learn about yourself?

   _____

   _____

   _____

   _____

   _____

   _____

   _____

2. What did you learn about your potential spouse?

   _____

   _____

   _____

   _____

   _____

   _____

13 AFTER THE WEDDING: SEXUAL RELATIONSHIP

"And from His signs is that He created from yourselves your spouses, that you find serenity with them, and He has set between you affection and mercy. Surely in this are signs for people who reflect."

Qur'an (30:21)

With years of secular schooling, American Muslims struggle between Islam and Western values that encourage dating and pre-marital sex. With films and television bombarding youth with messages about sex and relationships, Muslims undoubtedly adopt lofty and unrealistic expectations about love, sex and marriage. Up to this point in the book, prospective couples have discovered and explored their compatibility with regard to many subjects. This final section is for couples who have performed the marriage contract, as it pertains to a subject that is traditionally not covered until after marriage – their intimate life.

These questions will be difficult to ask and answer, so the couple should take their time and remember that even though they cannot talk about their sex life with other people, it does not mean that they should not talk about it with one another once married. The Prophet Muhammad (peace be upon him) was not shy when talking about sexual relations because he understood its importance in a happy marriage.

When Muslims get married, they are able to find solace in their spouse from a culture that is inundated with overt sexuality. Muslims may enter marriage with sexual frustrations and high expectations. Sexual incompatibility can cause a huge strain on a marriage. Expectations of the sexual relationship may not be viewed in the same way by each spouse, so it is important for the couple to communicate and understand each other's needs in order to have a satisfying sexual relationship. These questions will hopefully begin the conversation of exploring intimacy in the relationship for a healthy marriage.

1. How comfortable and willing are you discussing sex?

2. How did you first learn about sex? How was sex discussed in your family?

3. How important do you think sex is in our relationship?

4. How are you most comfortable expressing your affection?

5. Was your family affectionate toward one another? Are you comfortable expressing affection publicly?

6. What do you consider romantic? How can we build meaningful romance into our relationship?

7. Share a dream or fantasy you have.

8. How often do you wish to have sex? How do we cope when our desire levels do not match? What are your expectations?

9. What do you feel is the male/female responsibility to have a mutually satisfying and fulfilling sexual relationship?

10. What are your thoughts and views on oral sex?

11. What are your thoughts and views on masturbation?

12. How do you define pornography? Do you view pornography?

13. Are you comfortable expressing your desires and preferences sexually? How can we be more open with one another?

14. How does your body image affect our sexual relationship?

15. Do you feel that birth control is an individual or joint responsibility? What form of birth control do you prefer? Is there anything you are not willing to use?

TAKE A MOMENT

1. What did you learn about yourself?

___

2. What did you learn about your potential spouse?

___

14 THE MARRIAGE CYCLE

"All weddings are similar but every marriage is different."

-John Berger

The marriage relationship will change over time just as people naturally change over time. All marriages experience stressors that are so common they have been captured in what is known as the marriage relationship cycle. Since every relationship will be faced with difficulties it is empowering to understand the foreseeable challenges in order to be better prepared to deal with them when they occur. The different stressors can have a major impact on a relationship, so much so, that most divorces usually center around one of these common stressors. These stressors may not necessarily occur in a linear pattern but rather they may overlap or occur simultaneously.

Some of the stressors may be skipped over entirely for couples who do not have children.

Couples who best deal with stressors in their marriage are those who have built a strong foundation of commitment, mutual respect and compassion in their marriage. Couples that have the ability to be flexible and open to new ideas are also better able to engage new challenges in their relationship. Communication and problem solving skills will be tested as couples encounter these common stressors.

Wedding

The first stress point for new couples is the wedding. The process of wedding planning requires couples to compromise and resolve conflicts in order to accomplish their first task together, organizing the wedding day. Conflicts about family expectations and influence on the details of the wedding may come up at this time. Couples will need to discuss their desires and expectations for their wedding as well as decide on a budget of how much they plan to spend. Through this process the couple will begin to make joint decisions while at the same time communicate with their families so they are all included in the planning. This is also a time that couples begin to set boundaries with family members who may interfere in the couple's relationship. Despite the large amount of stress and negotiation required couples who continue to communicate and resolve conflicts as they arise will begin building a strong foundation to their marriage.

First Year of Marriage

When two people get married there is excitement and joy about their relationship and their future. The love they feel for one another is immeasurable and they may have an expectation that it will always be this way. Usually, in the first year of marriage the "rosy glasses" begin to fade and a couple begins to discover their unrealistic expectations about each other and about the relationship. They notice differences of opinion, annoying habits, particular preferences and differences in how they each handle situations. Also in this initial year they begin establishing their relationship roles by deciding how they will care for their home, manage their finances and spend their free time.

Stress occurs when they become aware of their unrealistic expectations and have difficulty adapting to the new reality. They face added stress if they cannot agree on their roles in the relationship. The "work" of marriage usually begins when the couple lets go of the unrealistic expectations and accepts their spouse as they truly are. The couple can then successfully navigate this stage in their relationship by actively committing to do what is best for "we" instead of what is best for "me." This shift creates deeper emotional investment in the relationship as they each learn to be flexible and seek to do what is best for their marriage and not only for themselves.

Birth of Child

The birth of the first child is usually an anticipated event for the couple and their families. With the new addition to the family comes the third stress point in the marriage. Up until the birth of the child, the relationship is centered around the needs of the couple and on their careers and education. When a child is born, the relationship shifts and becomes centered on the needs of the child. This is when the couple must begin to redefine their roles in the family as parents and as spouses. Decisions of who will be the primary caregiver of the child and any shift in their household roles will be negotiated. Stress during this stage occurs when the couple struggles to define their new roles, especially if they are different than the roles assumed by their own parents. Couples also learn to adjust to the demands of caring for children while making time for their relationship.

Couples who have a child and do not reach an agreement about the changing demands they will each face will have added stress. Couples that feel overwhelmed and unsupported in this stage can experience great stress if they do not share their feelings and expectations with their spouse. Couples who successfully navigate this stage are able to juggle the responsibility of caring for their child while at the same time nurturing their marriage. Couples who actively make time to emotionally connect with one another and prioritize their relationship build a stronger foundation. As parents they learn to lean on one another in the journey of parenting and find deeper love and support in their marriage as their family grows.

Raising Teenagers

The fourth stress point for married couples is when the children reach the teenage years. During this time, the couple experiences their teenager's identity development and a shift in their parenting responsibilities. Disagreements over parenting styles and poor communication between the couple can cause major stress. Couples may struggle to accept this new phase in their teen's life and stress occurs when the couple has become entirely focused on their teen's needs without taking time to nourish their relationship. Also, the couple at this time is dealing with their own midlife transition as they assess their life goals and past experiences. Couples who navigate this stage successfully are able to co-parent with mutual respect and have established a strong family system with solid support and encouragement. Couples who continue to make an effort to connect with one another and share their goals and aspirations have a strong emotional connection which better prepares them to launch their teen into their college years and adulthood.

Empty Nest

Once the children have moved out of the family home, the marriage relationship becomes couple-centered again. This transition may be positive or negative depending on the foundation of the marriage. For some couples, the children leaving, causes an "empty nest" feeling. The couple feels lost without the children and struggle to find new purpose. Couples who have not nurtured their relationship will experience loneliness and emotional distance from their spouse. For other couples, the opportunity to become refocused on their marriage is exciting. These couples look forward to spending time together and reinvesting in their relationship. Stress occurs during this period when the couple has emotionally grown apart and does not seek to develop new common interests together. If the couple does not work to renew their companionship by enjoying time together they will continue to drift apart. Couples who successfully navigate this stress point are committed to reinvesting in the marriage as they seek to create a lasting and fulfilling partnership into their senior years.

Aging Parents

Couples may spend as many years caring for

aging and ill parents as they spend caring for their own children. The sixth stress point for couples is the caretaking of an aging parent, especially if the parent moves into the family home. The emotional and financial demands of caretaking become stressful when the responsibility is not shared by both spouses or there are misaligned expectations. Discussing the changing demands on the family, seeking support and sharing personal feelings and expectations with one another will help the couple manage this stress point in the marriage. Additionally, the couple needs to work to maintain a couple-focused relationship by balancing time caring for an aging parent with time nurturing the marriage.

Senior Years

Finally, marriage in later life holds the possibility of being the happiest time couples can spend together. The attitude the couple has toward life and aging influences the relationship. The major stressor couples experience in this stage of the marriage are health problems, sadness at the loss of friends and family members and their increasing dependence on their children for care. Couples who maintain healthy life styles, participate in enjoyable activities together and have a positive attitude will enjoy a deep and meaningful life with one another.

The marriage stressors outlined are common

and all couples will endure them, some will grow because of them while others will crumble because of them. However, acknowledging the conflicts, engaging in joint problem solving and making a tireless commitment are some pathways for couples to overcome these stressors in their marriage.

Researchers have found that long lasting happy marriages all have similar traits. Couples consistently do the following three things: remain good friends, show kindness, and establish family traditions. These basic yet profound elements are what couples too often forget to do when they experience stress in their relationship.

Friendship

Remaining good friends is the foundation to a happy marriage. This requires couples to maintain mutual respect and love for one another through their words and actions. Sharing thoughts and feelings and having fun together – just as one would with a close friend – are vital in a marriage. Communicating with a spouse creates greater intimacy and this deeper bond helps sustain the couple even in times of difficulty. Through these moments of connection the couple turns to each other for love and encouragement and they exemplify being on the same "team," working toward similar goals.

Couples who laugh together, dream together and try new things together are happier because they truly enjoy each other's company. Deliberately planning time together is vital because so many couples are living hectic and busy lives. Scheduling outings or "date-nights" becomes even more important once the couple has children because it ensures the relationship does not get neglected. Making an effort to spend time together, doing something both spouses enjoy, needs to be a priority. Everything from simple activities like picnics, movies, and walks to more elaborate activities like vacations and all day outings are all ways couples build deeper intimacy and create new memories.

Acts of Kindness

Spouses find it easy to appreciate one another at the beginning of their relationship: they seek to please and show their affection through kind gestures and gifts. Kindness promotes love and romance in the marriage because it prevents the couple from taking each other for granted. Small daily acts of kindness are powerful because they keep little annoyances from being blown out of proportion. The respected research of Dr. John Gottman, found that happy couples have five positive encounters for every one negative. This atmosphere of positivity in the relationship then acts as a buffer against negative stressors the couple encounters. Positivity in the relationship is shown everyday through small acts of kindness. Emphasizing the positive aspects of the relationship and actively working to build positive encounters creates a happier marriage.

Couples who express their appreciation verbally to one another commonly say things like, "thank you," and "I love you" as well as give each other compliments. Other ways appreciation can be shown is through kind emails, notes, gifts and special surprises. Couples who commonly kiss, hug and touch one another have greater affection and care for one another. Helping and encouraging a spouse with their goals and dreams are ways of expressing kindness. Acknowledging and reciprocating kindness from a spouse develops love in the relationship and leads to the couple being happier.

Creating Traditions

Finally, creating family traditions gives deeper meaning and predictability to marriages and families. Couples who incorporate traditions into their marriage forge a deeper commitment to one another. Through small acts like calling one another daily, praying together, and having dinner together, they establish routines that keep them deeply connected to one another. The family traditions created around holiday celebrations and yearly vacations develops a sense of belonging and commitment to the family while also building lasting memories.

Understanding the stressors that will occur in most marriages as well as focusing on the protective factors to strengthen marriages are great tools for new couples to consider when embarking on their life together. Building a strong and happy marriage is more important than all other relationships. The companionship and tranquility a person can find with their spouse will not only last a lifetime but will *insha'Allah* continue into the hereafter. God reminds us in the Qur'an of the long term goal of our relationships with the following prayer, "O our Sustainer! Grant that our spouses and our offspring be a joy to our eyes, and cause us to be foremost among those who are conscious of you." (Qur'an 25:74)

TAKE A MOMENT

1. What stage is your marriage in?

_____

_____

_____

_____

_____

_____

2. How do you manage stressors in your marriage?

_____

_____

_____

_____

_____

15 INTERCULTURAL & INTERFAITH MARRIAGES

"O Mankind. Indeed We have created you from male and female and made you into nations and tribes so that you may know one another..."

Qur'an (49:13)

Muslims in America represent diverse ethnic and racial backgrounds and this has led to an increase in intercultural and interfaith marriages. Despite the taboo amongst parents in the Muslim community of marrying "outside" of one's race, culture or religion, there is an emerging trend of young couples marrying based solely on religion, disregarding culture or race, and yet other couples choosing to marry a spouse of a different religion altogether. These types of marriages can have stresses and strains beyond those experienced in most marriages because they have "built-in" differences in areas that are particularly sensitive to the families of origin, and will at times require extra effort from the couple in building bridges in order to create a strong and lasting marriage.

Of course, all couples, whether of the same background or not, will encounter differences in their marriage. Individuals come from different "family cultures," where roles and expectations were inherited and then transferred into their own marriage dynamics. Couples who were raised in the West may have similar cultural values even though their families of origin come from different cultures. Therefore, all couples must learn to manage and resolve their differences in a marriage even if they share the same cultural and religious background. However, when a relationship is interfaith and/or intercultural, couples must learn to be proactive because disagreements in their relationship may be broader as a result of their different inherited values.

Research has shown that three core areas have added challenges in intercultural and interfaith marriages. These three areas are: (1) Communication styles, (2) Extended family relationships and (3) Parenting practices.

A couple from different cultural backgrounds can face extra challenges when communicating and listening to one another. This is not necessarily because they don't speak the same language, but rather because cultures tend to impact the *manner* in which individuals express themselves. Depending on the upbringing, people will differ in how loudly and quickly they communicate, even if both husband and wife communicate in English. In addition, each individual's culture has shaped how she or he argues, teases, jokes and listens, as well as the idiosyncrasies and body language they use. Therefore, misunderstandings in communication because of varying language barriers or cultural nuances can cause conflict in marriages. A couple must learn to be sensitive to their partner's communication style as well as understand the influence their upbringing has had on how they communicate a message. Once a couple effectively learns their partner's "language of communication", they will be able to diminish conflicts in this area.

Sometimes interfaith and intercultural issues are apparent early on in the relationship, often emerging as early as the wedding planning and lasting as long as the in-laws are around. These differences can involve the expectations of couples' families of origin about the wedding ceremony or even influence over decisions. Couples may have differing attitudes regarding the role of their extended family in their marriage. Cultural values may dictate that in-laws must have a say in every decision surrounding the wedding or the couple may be expected to spend a specific amount of time with the in-laws once they are married. On the other hand, in-laws may be so deeply committed to their cultural identity that they are unable to appreciate the ways in which their adult child has adapted to the spouse's culture; therefore they may limit contact to the "foreign family" or never warm up to the spouse. When in-laws avoid the new couple for personal reasons, it can cause stress to the marriage and family. Also, when the couple has children they will need to determine the relationships the in-laws have with their grandchildren and consider wider cultural or religious values in their interactions with extended family.

Parenting practices can also bring friction for an intercultural or interfaith couple in making religious, educational or cultural decisions for their children. Generally, most married couples are surprised to learn that when they become parents they each have different ideas of how to parent. However, when a couple has added their diverse cultural or religious values, they may find very different perceptions of how they feel their children should behave and be raised.

Areas such as which 'mother tongue' or mainstream language the children will learn, which holidays will be celebrated, and how faith will be transferred to the child, must be discussed before having children or even before marrying in order to reduce potential conflicts in the marriage. In addition, areas of discipline, expectations of appropriate gender behavior and teaching children manners are very much culturally derived, therefore couples need to compromise and determine what their own family vision will be once they have children. Conflicts can arise if a spouse feels their culture or religion is being devalued, or one spouse does not respect both their heritages nor share a mutual respect of their family backgrounds. Raising children with an appreciation for two cultures and two faiths can be enriching, but it can only happen if couples communicate their ideas and values with one another.

Problems and conflicts in intercultural and interfaith marriages are often because of assumptions and expectations that are made by the individual and couple. These expectations are infused into a person's identity through their life experiences and family background. Individuals preparing for marriage are usually not even consciously aware of their unrealistic expectations and any potential conflicts that can occur in the marriage because of their culture or religion. Before a couple can decide how their beliefs and values will mesh with one another they must individually explore their core beliefs and values in order to gain self-awareness of their personal identity. Once an individual is aware of what is most important to them personally they will be able to communicate with their spouse what type of family they envision raising their children in and better compromise their cultural and religious backgrounds to enrich their family life.

Dr. Joel Crohn explains in his book, *Mixed Matches: How to Create Successful Interracial, Interethnic, and Interfaith Relationships* five basic patterns for managing cultural, racial and religious differences in a marriage Intercultural and interfaith couples will go through any one of these patterns as they establish their family vision:

1) Transcendent: The couple adopts beliefs, traditions and rituals from multiple sources, including ones outside the cultures, races and religions of their origin. The couple's spiritual practices may be nontraditional. This pattern is usually found with a couple that was not raised with any strong religious or cultural background and so they seek to create their own. This pattern is not typical of Muslim families as they have distinct religious and/or cultural values that they enter a marriage with and learn to compromise.

2) Secular: The couple takes a nonreligious approach to life and is minimally involved in the practice of cultural and religious beliefs, rituals and traditions. This pattern is evident in Muslim families

and can emerge with couple's who do not have strong ties to their religious background and may have weak ties to their cultural background. This approach does not encourage a development of culture or religion within the family practices nor in raising the children.

3) Bi-cultural: The couple tries to balance the beliefs, traditions and rituals from each partner's cultural, religious and racial backgrounds. If there are two languages, the children will probably speak both. This pattern is common in many Muslim families as they seek to incorporate both cultures and infuse the language, food, dress and traditions of both cultures to their children. The couple appreciates and celebrates both spouse's heritages. Within this pattern it may be difficult for families to balance both cultures and place an equal emphasis on both cultures indistinguishably.

4) Modified Bi-cultural: The couple adopts a single religion, either from one partner's background or a mutually agreeable "compromised" religion and tries to honor the beliefs and traditions of both partners in a selective, but relatively balanced way. If there are two languages, the children may or may not speak both. This pattern is most common in Muslim families, where the child is raised with the Islamic faith and the couple compromises on the cultural practices that the family adopts with mutual respect for their family heritages and traditions and openness to creating new traditions. The balance that the couple

strives towards, in this pattern, is practical as it is encourages the couple to compromise in developing their family traditions and a respect for culture is maintained.

5) Assimilated: One partner assimilates and converts to the beliefs, traditions and rituals of the other partner's cultural, religious and racial background. This pattern can also be seen in many Muslim families where one spouse lets go of their religious or cultural background and completely adopts their spouses traditions. In the case of spouse's that convert to Islam, there also is a letting go of their cultural background many times seeing it as "un-Islamic," rather than adopting the positive cultural practices into their family traditions. Other couples will negate one spouse's culture completely and adopt the dominant culture (i.e. Arab or Indo-Pakistani) into their family traditions through food, dress and celebrations. This pattern requires little compromise and lacks the concept of mutual respect for each spouse's heritage nor does it give children an opportunity to celebrate both cultures of the parents.

All couples, despite cultural and religious convictions will negotiate differences when entering a marriage. This is because two individuals come from two different families, and as a couple they will develop their own family identity by choosing the traditions, habits and beliefs they value and want to celebrate in their family and with their own children. The process of forming a family is more complex for couples of different cultures and religions. Yet, despite these complex challenges, successful intercultural and interfaith relationships have many personal benefits. Couples who are willing to manage differences with each other and their respective families generally promote communities that have more integrated identities and a greater appreciation for diversity. This process however, does not happen automatically; a successful and diverse marriage takes personal work and sensitivity to self and others. The rewards then are immeasurable.

Munira Lekovic Ezzeldine, "Intercultural and Interfaith Marriages" www.suhaibwebb.com. Copyright © 2010-2013. All rights reserved. Reproduced with permission.

ABOUT THE AUTHOR

Munira Lekovic Ezzeldine is a trained Prepare/Enrich facilitator and has been providing pre-marital counseling services to couples since 2008. She received her M.S. in Marriage and Family Counseling from California State University, Fullerton and her B.S. from the University of California, Los Angeles in Economics.

Ezzeldine has written two Islamic Studies textbooks for the Bureau of Islamic and Arabic Education. She contributed a chapter in the books *Modern Muslim Marriage* and *Muslims in America: Contemporary Issues*. She was a monthly columnist for *Muslim Girl Magazine* and *www.SuhaibWebb.com*. She co-hosted the radio show *Family Connection* on One Legacy Radio where she discussed topics about family, marriage and children. She has been happily married for over fifteen years and the mother of three amazing sons. She is currently writing her next book.

Made in the USA
San Bernardino, CA
30 November 2016